DISCARD

795 40/1

D1165034

DESIGNING WITH STRING

DESIGNING WITH STRING

Mary Seyd

B T Batsford Ltd   London

Watson-Guptill Publications   New York

© Mary Seyd 1967

First published 1967
Reprinted 1969 (twice)

7134 2260 2

Library of Congress Catalog Card Number 68–10049

Made and printed in Great Britain by
William Clowes and Sons Ltd, London and Beccles
for the Publishers
B T BATSFORD LIMITED
4 Fitzhardinge Street London W1 and
WATSON-GUPTILL PUBLICATIONS
165 West 46th Street New York NY 10036

CONTENTS

710304

ACKNOWLEDGMENT

I wish first to thank Miss Thelma Nye of B T Batsford Ltd for suggesting that there was sufficient in this subject to justify research. I have enjoyed discovering how right she was!

I am much indebted to students, past and present of Sidney Webb College, who have contributed their own work and used this medium with children from nursery age upwards. For their enthusiastic response I am tremendously grateful, and only sorry that limited space made it impossible to use more of the work submitted.

I am grateful to lecturers at Colleges of Education and Schools of Art, who have generously sent photographs and colour transparencies and parcels of their students' work, as well as their own. I would thank especially Miss Ivy Haley (Hereford College of Education, now at the Lady Spencer-Churchill College); Mrs Elisa Rees (Cardiff College of Art); Miss Ann Croot (Stourbridge College of Art); Miss Mabel Huggins (Avery Hill College of Education); Mrs Susan James (Mid-Warwickshire College of Further Education, School of Art) and Mrs Nancy Duckworth (Farnham School of Art—Saturday Childrens' Class). Also may thanks to Mrs Parker (Constance Howard) of Goldsmiths College, School of Art, for her encouragement and help.

I am particularly grateful to Mr Peter Collingwood, and *The Handweaver and Craftsman*, for allowing me to reproduce part of an article on 'Sprang', also to Mr Collingwood for photographs of work by Ann Sutton and Ruth Hurle, which are in his private collection, as well as his own work.

I would also thank other friends of long-standing who have lent me examples of their work, or encouraged their children to experiment with string and rope.

My thanks and gratitude to The Whitechapel Art Gallery for information, and to Gimpel Fils Ltd for permission to reproduce work by Gwyther Irwin; to Dr B Hodek of Artia, Prague, for allowing me to use illustrations from *Life Under the Microscope;* to my friends Michael Thompson and David Guppy of Studex Photography, who took the photographs of work by Sidney Webb students and their classes. Without their photographic skill and efficiency this book could hardly have begun; my thanks also to my husband for photographs at home and abroad, without which it could never have been concluded.

Grayshott 1967

M S

INTRODUCTION

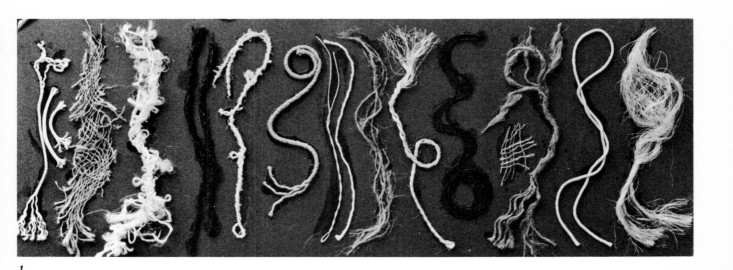

1

The idea for this book arose as part of a larger scheme on the value of inexpensive and scrap materials for beginning creative work. For this reason the term 'string' is very loosely applied to cover all kinds of tying and working fibres, with emphasis on those which are readily available. In the examples shown in the final chapter, this is less important, for here work represents more sophisticated art forms. However, in the early stages it matters that the material itself is ordinary and replaceable, though full of variety, and costs little. The would-be artist can relax and be playful, not minding if the first experiments come to nothing. So often the expense of the initial outlay inhibits experiment and discovery which is so essential to original work.

The dictionary defines string as 'Twine or fine cord; a length of this *or some other material* serving to tie or attach or work something'. Twisted cellophane, paper or wool and indeed any fibre that has unique qualities could all in this context be termed string.

In every medium we choose to explore, we must first investigate the nature of the material. This process is so basic and so vital to a right use of the material that the importance of this investigation cannot be overstressed. The principle is indisputable, yet too many craft teachers still leave out this stage of exploration, and jump right in with an exercise, a picture or 'something useful'. If a great deal of exploration has taken place at the infant and junior stages, it is usually possible to devise more ingenious forms of investigation with older children and adult beginners. The latter will be very lucky if they were encouraged to play purposefully in their youth.

In her book *Creative Craft in Education*, Seonid Robertson quotes a teacher who wanted to teach her class about weaving. She began by giving the children pieces of cloth to pull apart, and asked them what they noticed, what clue it gave as to how the cloth was made. They noticed that strands in one direction were straight and in the other they bumped evenly up and down. They decided that one set of strands had been held tight and the other threaded in between. The teacher then asked the children if they could invent a way of doing this with wool. The children eventually invented practically every known form of primitive loom, and were enormously impressed when she showed them a heddle, which solved the problem they had found most difficult.

This is a digression to underline the value of beginning at the beginning. Here we are concerned with string and rope. We begin with all we can collect or buy, from the finest corded string to thick rope, made of all sorts of materials. These include hemp, sisal, linen, paperwaste, asbestos and nylon. They serve all manner of purposes, such as parachute cord, binder-twine, gardening string (smelling of creosote), fine cord for elegant parcels or rough sisal for bedding hamsters. What an interesting project a teacher could develop from this collection alone; and how much better the children might remember the facts of world geography if the by-products of their explorations—pulling the string apart to notice how much one sort varied from another—could also be mounted in a way that they would remember.

The following pages illustrate the variety of patterns that can arise from simple un-winding, teasing, chopping, twisting and lightly sticking down. The first examples are from one kind of rope or string, at first merely pulled apart, later twisted and plaited (braided), looped and coiled, chopped into pieces of different lengths or kept as one continuous length. Since the variations on one material alone are considerable, the possibilities in combination with other kinds are infinite. Perhaps because of this, some of the most subtle and sensitive compositions in string confine themselves to using one kind alone, worked in one consistent manner. There is a temptation when one begins and gets excited with the possibilities, as in so many crafts, to attempt too much, and so be too clever and too complicated.

1   THE MATERIALS

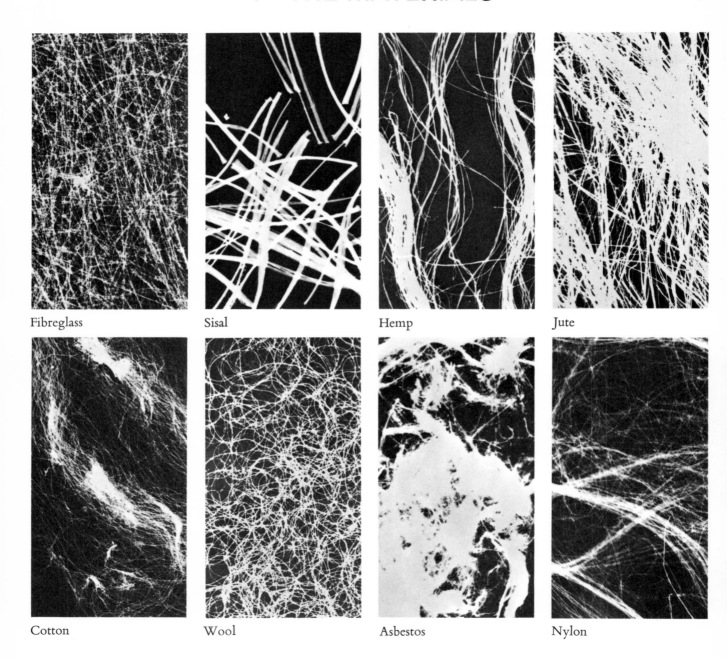

Fibreglass

Sisal

Hemp

Jute

Cotton

Wool

Asbestos

Nylon

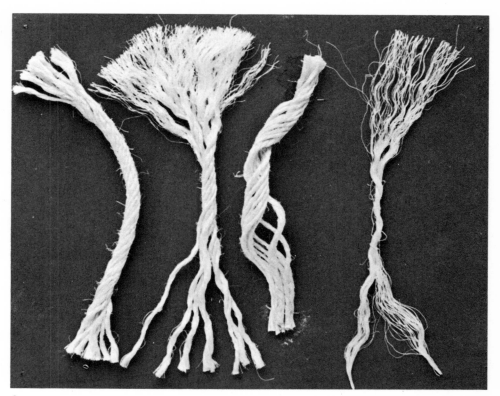

3

Sisal (2, 5 and 16)

Sisal comes from the fleshy blade-like leaves of *agave sisalana*. The fibres are hard, creamy-white, springy and stiff like horsehair. From these come the commonest form of packaging string, which is therefore cheap and easy to collect. Unravelled, the ends spring apart.

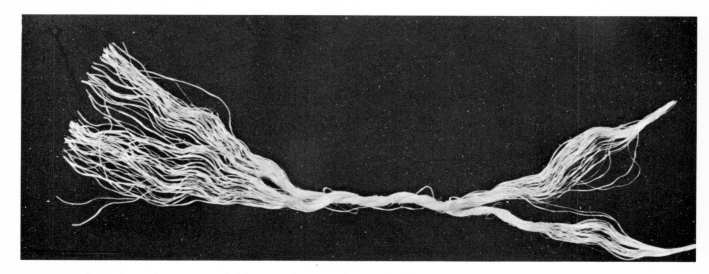

4 Here the ends are shown twisted, like waxed moustaches, with glue. In this case a strong wallpaper paste was used. Below, binder twine, also made from sisal and sisal string, is shown contrasted, unravelled and curled.

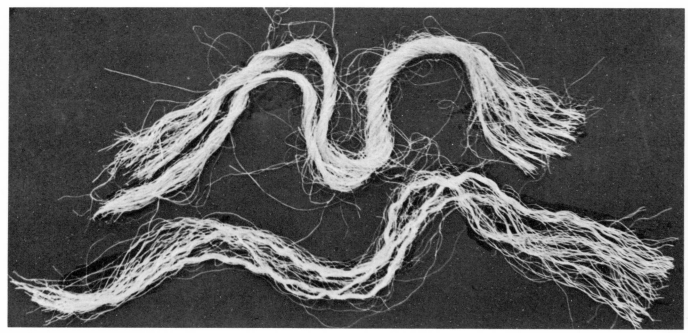

5

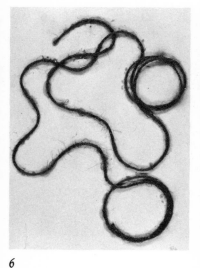

6

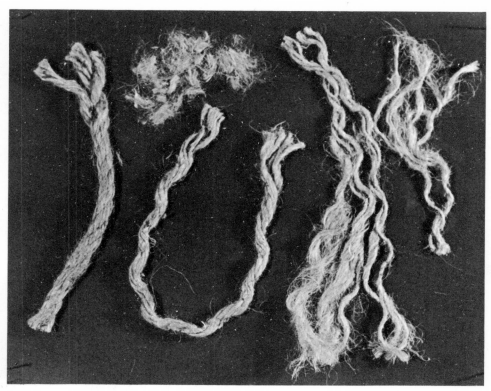

8

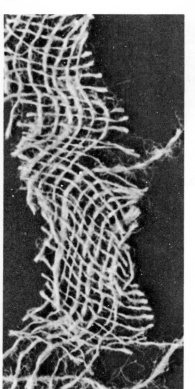

7

Manilla

This fibre is very similar to sisal to look at, though whiter and in fact stronger. It comes from *acaba* and before the war we imported more manilla than sisal. It is used for good quality ropes and string, being the strongest natural fibre produced in quantity.

Jute (*2, 6-8, 15* and *16*)

Jute comes from the inner bark of a tall plant—*corchorus*. Sackcloth is perhaps its commonest form now, and many sorts of webbing, rope and twine, including tarred garden and marine twine. Compared with sisal it appears limp, matted, soft brown and less strong. It unravels into an untidy web which can be very decorative.

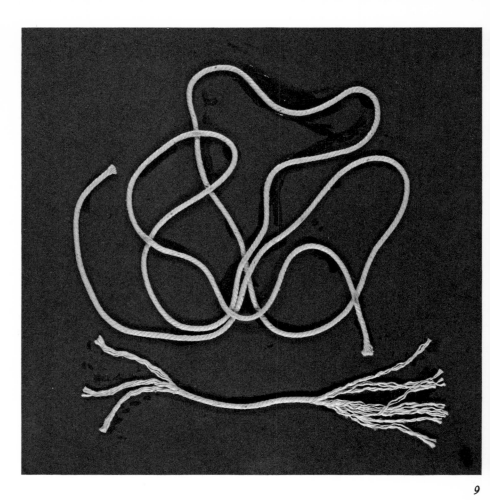

9

Cotton (*2* and *9*)

Cotton fibres come from the 'bol', the pod or seed-head of the cotton plant. This grows in warm climates, as do also sisal and jute, but the fibres are soft and white—hence 'cotton wool'. We recognise them in loosely spun lint and dishcloth yarn and more tightly spun in good quality white twine, both fine and thick. It also makes soft handling ropes. All these forms loop easily and unravelled the strings make neat frizzy trails.

Linen

Linen, the oldest of our native fibres, comes from the stems of flax. More cream in colour and harsher than cotton, it is used for strong threads by tailors, shoemakers, sail-makers, bookbinders and upholsterers. Linen is used more now for cloth than for string or rope, as man-made fibres are stronger and cheaper to produce.

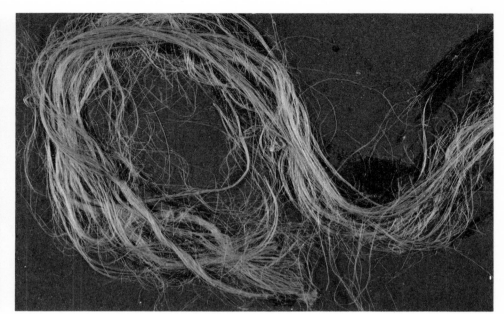

11

1

10

Hemp (2 and 11)

Hemp is another soft fibre, like jute, but finer and lighter in colour. It comes from the stems of *cannabis sativa*, a plant of the same family as hops. It is greyish or yellow according to the method used for 'retting'. The stems are either left in the open for the soft part to rot away in the dew (dew-retting) or else they are steeped in water tanks for the same thing to happen (water-retting). The former fibres are grey and the latter yellowish. Hemp is often used as a substitute for linen, and for about twenty centuries was the principal fibre used in ropes. Sisal and jute gradually replaced it and now man-made fibres are assisting these. Hemp is still used for strong tying twines, sacking and bookbinders twine and for carpet warp, canvas and sail. British readers will probably recognise it best as the silken and flaxy looking plumbers' tow.

Coir

Coir, from coconut husk, is still used for cheap rope for fishing boats and rough sailing. It is made from the hard and hairy brown fibres of the husk that surrounds the coconut.

Asbestos (2 and 10)

Asbestos has some of the same lumpy quality of coir rope but the fibrous particles are whitish-grey and twisted together to make ropes and webbing that are incombustible. It is not advisable for teachers to use asbestos in any quantity as the particles inhaled can be poisonous. Asbestos fibre is made from a mineral that is mined from rock, mainly in Canada but also in other parts of the world.

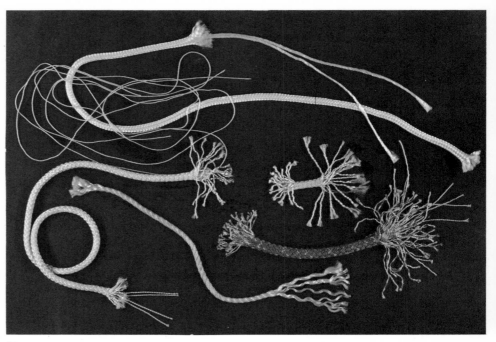

12

Paper string

This is one of the cheapest kinds of string, made of brown twisted paper. Easily break-able and quickly sodden in water, it is the poorest kind of string imaginable but never-theless has decorative possibilities which could be exploited.

Nylon and Terylene (2 and 12)

These man-made fibres are rot-proof and unpalatable even to insects. They are also resistant to chemical action owing to their molecular structure, and are extremely strong. The filaments are continuous, which is something not possible in any natural fibre, and for this reason they are ousting the natural fibres wherever strength is the essential quality needed. Shining and immaculately woven, pulled apart nylon makes superb tangles. The centres of woven nylon cord and rope are packed solid with fine nylon threads, each spun of many long fibres which are chains of elongated cells. Nylon ropes have a high stretch as well as strength and are used for absorbing shock loads.

Terylene on the other hand gives low stretch plus strength. Pre-stretched it is used for ropes under constant tension. For easy handling it can be given a furry matt finish, like cotton. For depth-plumbing it can be woven with the yarns of the rope strands twisted in the opposite direction to the final twist of the strands of the rope. This makes the length of the rope stay constant instead of shrinking in the water.

13

Polypropylene
   Polypropylene is a lightweight, inexpensive commercial rope, not as strong as terylene but likely eventually to replace manilla and sisal. To look at, it is similar to sisal, but whiter and it floats, as do also *ulstron* and *courelle* which are versions of polypropylene.

Fibreglass (*2* and *14*)

Here the basic fibres are extremely fine and can be spun into cloth or used with acrylic resin to make a material as strong as steel, for such things as car bodies and boats. Compressed into slabs for ceilings it is decorative as well as functional for heat insulation. Artistically, because of its translucency, it has interesting possibilities; woven into cloth it makes washable, non-iron, translucent fabric.

Cellophane

Interesting experiments can be done with non-sticky cellophane, flat, twisted or plaited (braided). It can be used over a tie-dyed warp so that the transparency of the weft threads show through the pattern of the warp thread. Cellophane adds sparkle as well as transparency (*112*).

Wool and Animal Hair

These have been left to the end because there are so may varieties. They could be the subject of a book on their own. Wool's essential nature, whether long or short staple, is its springiness, as the enlarged photograph clearly shows. In contrast to all other fibres, its softness and springiness make it less suitable than vegetable fibres for most tying purposes and it is easily broken, though it has an important place in embroidery, rug-making and weaving.

This gives some idea of the variety of substances that comprise our most used strings, ropes, cords, twines, yarns and threads. There are a great variety of processes of twisting and plaiting (braiding). In rope-making, threads are twisted into yarns (spinning), the yarns are laid together in a spiral twist to form the strands, and the strands twisted around each other to complete the rope. So if we proceed to unwind and open up the threads, or to twist or manoeuvre together in new ways, the possibilities are almost infinite.

2 PLAYING WITH THE MATERIAL

Different kinds of string have their individual ways of parting and curling or springing. Some are soft and limp, some are strong and springy. Sisal unwinds easily and makes hair loops like the seed-pods of willow herb or tufts like fishermen's beards. It was the way the sisal binder twine curled without any forcing that suggested the composition *Seed Dispersal* (*63*). This principle of following the nature of the material without forcing it into a preconceived pattern is basic to sound craftsmanship. It is the reason why exploration and understanding precede use in any other way. It is easy to torture the material to a too literal idea. The consequent results can be clever but insensitive. This temptation is avoided by allowing the qualities of the material to remain more important than any pictorial idea that may arise. The successful 'picture' arises in a seemingly effortless way from the materials that comprise it. It is often best to use only one material at first and see how far you can take it. This involves the string shapes alone in relation to the ground to which it is stuck or sewn—an excercise in space relations. Alternatively the whole background can be covered and liveliness introduced by means of various thicknesses and textures. The variations with one material alone are enormous. Perhaps the most sophisticated examples in this book are the 'paintings' of Gwyther Irwin (*66* and *108*).

Jute, unlike sisal, makes untidy knotty loops and peepholes. Sisal and jute rope, slightly unwound may easily suggest a wood in winter. The shininess of tangled nylon may evoke pictorial images or form a focal point in an abstract composition. There are endless ways in which string can be plaited (braided), knotted, crochetted, knitted, woven, looped, coiled, bunched, twisted and chopped. Each kind of string responds to these processes in quite different ways.

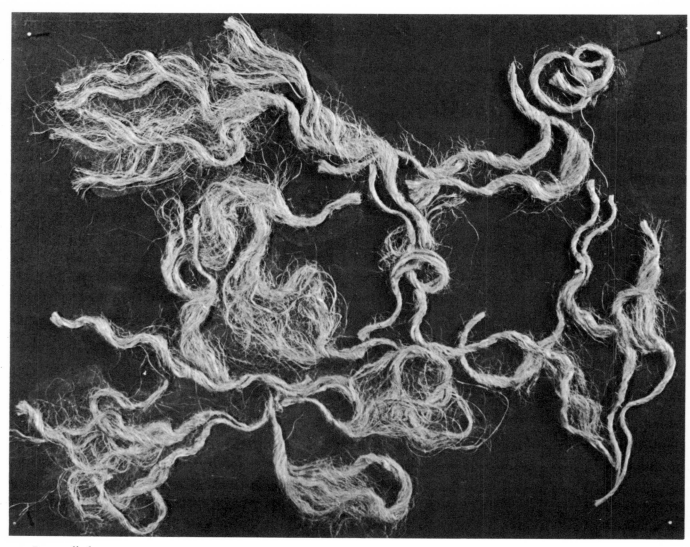

15 Jute pulled apart

16 Jute and sisal pulled apart

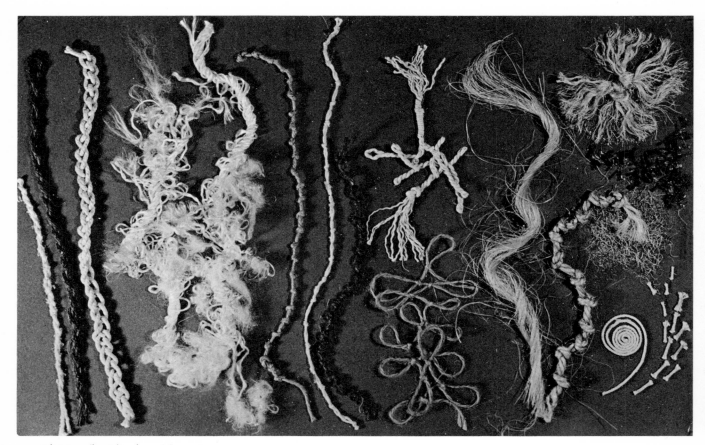

17 Plaiting (braiding) and knotting

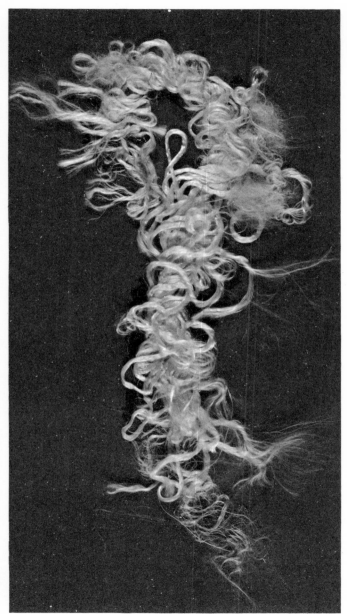

19 An example of how different various strings appear when chopped

18 Nylon tangled up

Already this sort of play is leading to space-filling exercises where the shape area of the string has to be considered in relation to the shape and area of the background. Are the spaces between considered as carefully as the shapes and rhythms of the string? Are they related, balanced, echoed? Is there sufficient contrast of large shapes and small? Is there unity? These are the questions that arise at this stage as we decide on the arrangement and stick the string to the background. Of course it is possible also to play in space and doodle in three dimensions. This development is dealt with in *Creative Textile Craft: Thread and Fabric* by Rolf Hartung.

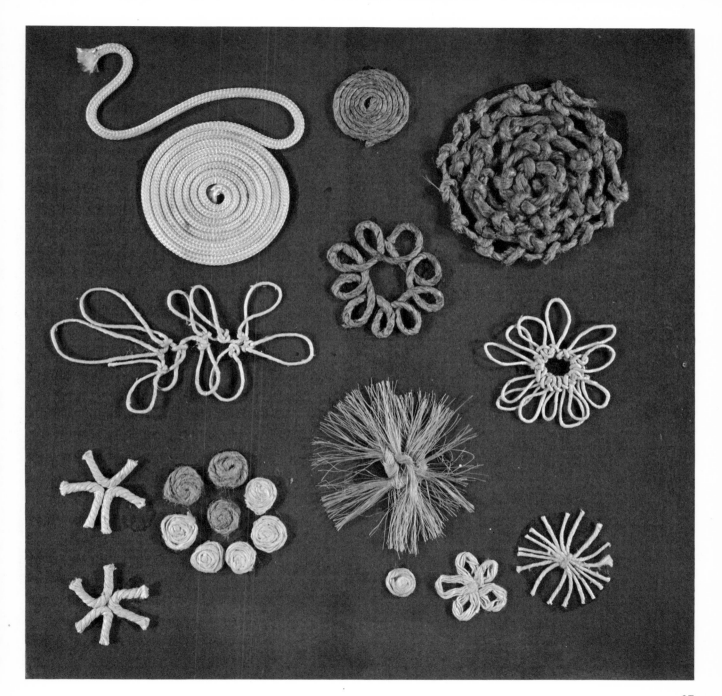

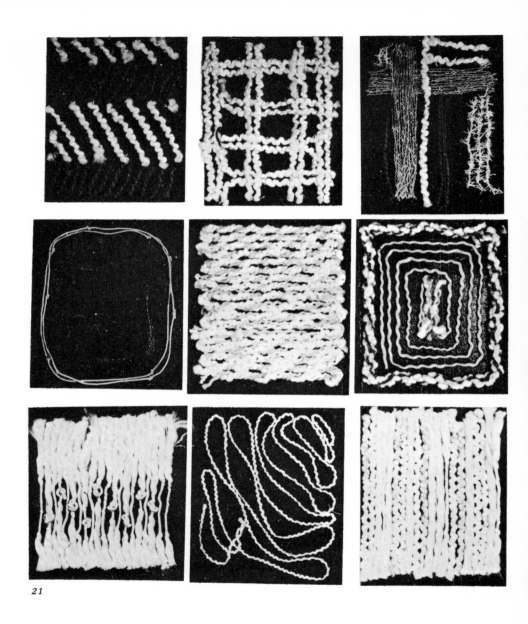

21

21   Variations on a square theme made by students of weaving from a college of art

22 *opposite*   Another circular motif by the same students

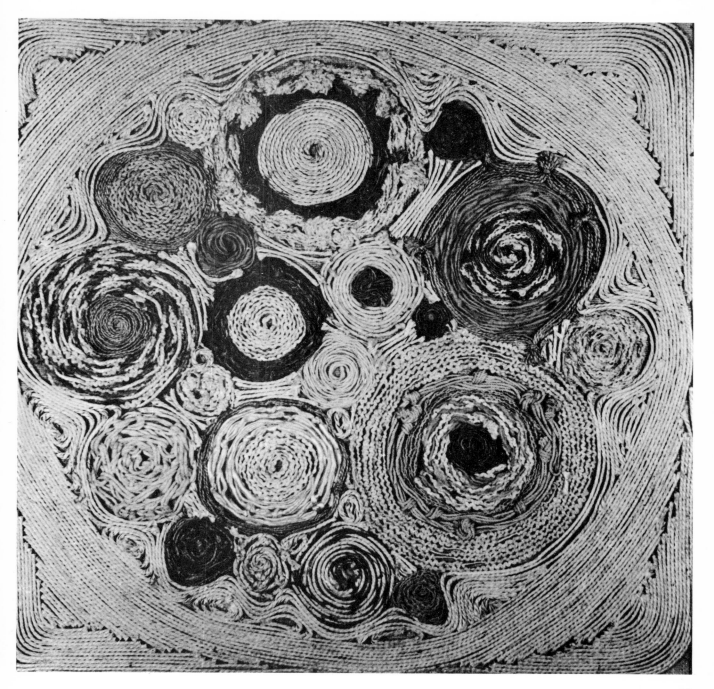

23 An exercise based on circles by a student of embroidery at a college of education

3 ADHESIVES AND GROUNDS

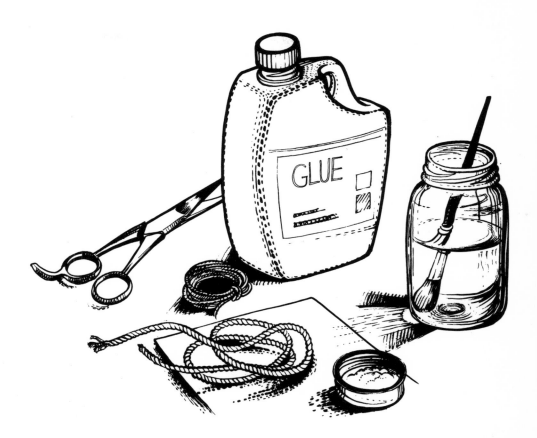

There are a great many kinds of string; there are also many kinds of adhesive which may be used to stick them down and a variety of grounds to which they may be stuck. These range from thick paper, cardboard, hardboard or strawboard, to canvas, cloth or weaving warp, and other grounds could be invented—a web of string could be woven in space, or transparent nylon threads could act as a base, or netting. Inventing new means is part of the process. Gwyther Irwin's fine cord (66) is stuck with transparent polyvinyl acetate (pva) adhesive, or white glue, to stretched canvas. A weaving warp, either set up on a loom or on a weaving-frame of a more primitive type, such as a card-loom, would make an ideal ground for experiments. The warp itself could be made of threads of varying thicknesses. Cloth backgrounds which have an affinity to the fibres used are suitable. Sackcloth, vegetable netting, coarse linen, hessian (burlap) of various subtle and beautiful colours, including black: all these can be effective with natural rope and string. The man-made fibres may be more effective on material woven from fibreglass, nylon or terylene. Here perspex (Plexiglas) and plastic have a place. Plastic tubing bound with translucent or shining threads could give depth to a composition (*84*).

Of adhesives, the various forms of pva are strongest and most satisfactory. They come under trade names and are all milky, white, viscous fluids, soluble in water until set, afterwards transparent and extremely strong. There is a certain 'shuffling-time' which can be an advantage, but when set it will hold not only thick rope, but also shells, pebbles and chunks of metal or rock. Brushes should be rinsed in water, and it is advisable to keep a water-pot near while working and a damp sponge on which to wipe your fingers. Spots on clothes can be washed off with water provided this is done right away.

Thicker ropes may need weighting down until the adhesive sets, and in many cases a quicker setting adhesive may be preferred. For sticking to plastics special adhesives are necessary.

As small children will inevitably lick their fingers, care should be taken to purchase through an educational supplier an adhesive which is not harmful to them.

Sewing can be done stretched over a large frame or with the work flat on a table or board. Part may be done on a machine. A swing-needle sewing machine is valuable for this work, but an interesting contrast can be made by straightforward machine stitching combined with string couched on by hand.

The decorative possibilities can be explored by using warp threads on a loom as a ground. These warp threads can be woven together, keeping the warp tight and parallel, or they can be pulled out of parallel to make holes between of more varied shapes. Ruth Hurle's composition shows the variety of string textures that can be presented on a warp (*111*).

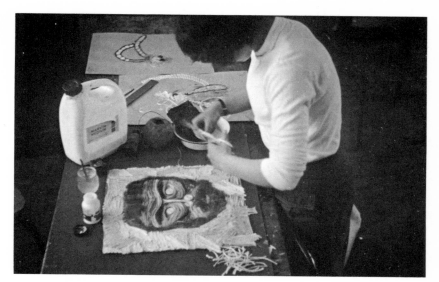

24 Sticking string on a card ground

25 Planning a string collage

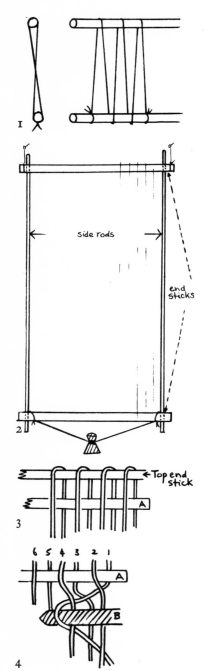

Sprang

Peter Collingwood, one of England's most distinguished weavers, has revived the ancient technique of *Sprang*, or Egyptian Plaitwork, which, used as wall-hangings, has many possibilities still to be explored. Utilitarian examples of this craft have been found in the Swiss Lake cultures, in the Danish Bronze Age burials, in Peru and in the Coptic finds in Egypt. The oldest are the Danish, and these show such mastery of the technique that it can only be supposed that Sprang was in existence long before these burials. It is still found amongst primitive people in India and South America, and visitors to Mexico now purchase hammocks and shopping bags made in this way.

Sprang is a net-like textile made by twisting together a set of warp threads held between an upper and a lower stick, no weft of any kind being used. The twists are pushed up and down the warps so that whatever pattern is being produced appears simultaneously at both ends of the warp, meeting eventually at the centre where some kind of fastening has to take place.

Sprang can be stretched in all directions. Unless it is held taut it collapses into a closely packed mass of threads with no visible design. For this reason a rigid frame which can be shortened in length as the work proceeds, has to be devised. One method is to attach two pieces of dowel ($\frac{1}{2}$ in.) temporarily to a fixed frame greater in length than the required finished length of sprang. Then tie an end of the warp yarn to one of the sticks and carry the warp alternately over the 2 sticks in a figure of eight (see diagram 1). Let the final tie be on the same stick as the starting tie. Remove the two sticks from the frame and hang the upper one at convenient working height. Weight the bottom one. The sticks should have holes bored at each end, parallel to the warp. Next a narrow metal rod is passed down through the holes on either side to make side supports (see diagram 2). The weight should hold these in place, but if it does not, these should be attached at the top only, so that they slide down as the work shortens.

A simple 1/1 twist sprang weave is done as follows:

1   Thread a stick, A, across the top of the warp in a plain weave shed, beginning with the right-hand thread *behind* the stick (diagram 3).

2   Put a second stick, B, across (below the first) from right to left and in the following manner. Take a loop of the first thread under the second, over the third, and under the fourth and put it over the end of the stick (diagram 4). Then take a loop of the third thread under the fourth, over the fifth, under the sixth and put it over the end of the

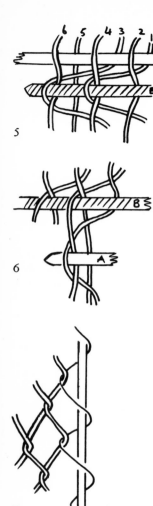

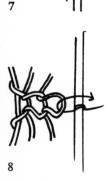

stick (diagram 5). Continue right across in this way. In this process the left hand picks up and manipulates the loops, the right hand slides the stick in.

At the end of the row, if there is an even number of threads in the warp, you will find there are two threads together *under* the stick at the right edge of the warp and two threads together *over* the stick at the left edge. The two right-hand threads can be seen in diagram 5 (the second and fourth).

3 Remove the first stick, A, and push B upwards forcing the twists up to the top. Take a third stick, C, put it in the same shed as B. Push C down the warp, forcing the twists down to the bottom. This movement explains why there are identical twists at top and bottom and why the fabric grows from its two ends to meet in the centre.

4 Take up stick A again and go across with it as in stage 2 above. But this time the beginning is slightly different due to the two threads together at the right-hand edge. Diagram 6 shows how the first loop is picked up; thereafter the process is the same as before and it continues right across. Note that at the end of this stage the threads are back in the order in which they started and that there are no double threads at either edge.

5 Remove B. Push A upwards. Remove C. Put it into A's shed and push C downwards.

Repeating stages, 2, 3, 4, 5 ad lib gives the single 1/1 twist, the simplest form of sprang.

After each repeat of this sequence secure the outermost thread on each side to the side rod by tying with cotton. Note that it is always the same thread which is attached each time (diagram 7). These ties can be replaced, when the piece is finished, by a continuous thread either of the warp material or of a very fine almost invisible material such as monofil nylon.

As the work proceeds, the piece naturally shortens due to the twistings and crossings of the warp, so the bottom stick is gradually rising all the time, sliding up the side rods. The weight on the stick must not be too heavy to prevent this.

Eventually the sprang fabric, growing from top to bottom, meets in the centre if so desired. Here, there must be some sort of fastening to prevent the whole fabric from untwisting. The normal method is to loop each thread through its neighbour, as the last stick is being withdrawn (diagram 8). Tie the last loop to secure this fastening.

Figure *27* shows a hanging made entirely of single 1/1 twist sprang and openings of various sizes. This combination holds great possibilities, and, since it is also technically simple, it is a good type for a beginner.

An opening is made by simply leaving untouched two threads which would normally be crossed and put on the stick. Referring back to diagram 5, the first thread is crossed behind the fourth, the third behind the sixth, the fifth behind the eighth and so on. This is normal 1/1 twist sprang. But if the third and sixth threads were left uncrossed (the third lying over the stick, the sixth behind it) an opening would begin at this point.

In the next row, the part of the fabric on each side of the opening is treated as a separate piece of sprang and worked accordingly.

In the next, the third row, the opening can be closed by crossing the third thread under the sixth in the normal way. This will of course give a very small opening. But the opening can be prolonged by leaving the third and sixth threads uncrossed for any *even* number of rows. Due to the elastic nature of the fabric an opening thus prolonged gapes wider and wider. The two large central openings in the photograph are the result of two threads being left uncrossed for 22 rows.

The photograph also illustrates another interesting characteristic of the technique. Because the fabric is stretchable the crossings and openings produced in one row alter and distort those that have gone before and are themselves altered and distorted by what follows. For instance, across the top of the hanging, there are really five small openings with four larger ones in between. But the various forces acting on the threads have practically obliterated three of the small openings and tilted the larger ones.

So there is an interaction between all the parts of the fabric and no element assumes its final shape or position until the very last row is worked. It is this interaction which converts the fairly mechanical sprang manipulations into a fabric with an altogether organic look—like a cross-section of some cellular structure.

This describes the method whereby one warp thread is twisted with one other warp thread. There can be double, treble and multiple twists, and threads can also be crossed without twisting. It rests with the experimenter to invent new variations of this cats' cradle type of weaving.

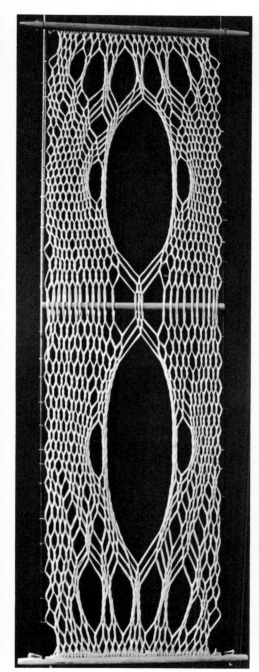

27

28

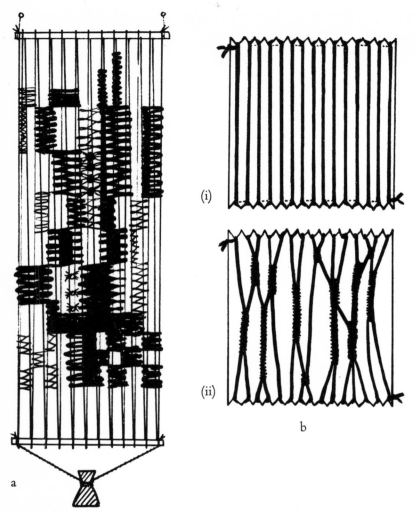

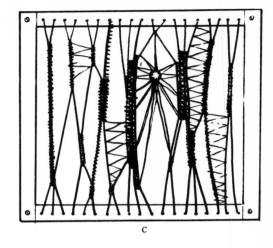

*Suggestions for working freely on a warp base using improvised frames,
tying and needle-weaving*

    (a)   Two poles and figure of eight warp—weighted at base
    (b)   Cardboard loom
        (i)   Threaded
        (ii)   Varying the spaces
    (c)   Wooden frame with holes drilled (ends are eventually cut and tied)

4 CHILDREN EXPERIMENT WITH STRING

Small children like to explore and experiment with every kind of material. String and rope, which are so easily available, need be no exception. The range of textures can be exciting and satisfying, and the bigger the range the better. It would be best at first to allow great freedom of choice, including other things such as buttons and seeds. A child may wish to experiment with one kind only, but at this stage aesthetics need not play a big part. It is enough to give choice and to refrain, if possible, from suggesting a subject. Although children may later use string as a line with which to draw a picture, the free patterns that arise from bits and pieces being stuck down are more to be expected, and these spacefilling exercises can be repeated at all stages. The teacher who suggests a subject too early may prevent the child from feeling free to explore the abstract textural qualities of the material. It is so easy for the child to go on thinking that string is the stuff with which to draw pictures because that is 'what teacher asked us to do with it'. At a later stage pattern-making or space-filling may seem babyish because it seems less 'clever'. Cleverness too easily replaces sensitivity as an aim.

The young children who made the compositions shown in figures *29–34* were so thrilled and so possessive of their creations that they had to repeat the exercise before their teacher dared ask if she could keep some to be photographed! They were perfectly content to stick their string on to pieces of black cardboard. Hannah, aged 3, was not happy with just string and stuck on buttons as well. She also chopped the edge of her card to make a more interesting shape (*34*).

Figures *35–38* are the work of a group of 5-year-olds who went on to do 'self portraits'.

In a group of 7-year-olds, Colin has written his name in unravelled string (*41*) while the rest enjoyed spreading the string over the background, filling up the space. Timothy and Simon, aged 7 and 9 respectively, were happy to 'doodle' with string and wool, but the background was creamy-white and it looked unattractive so they painted dabs of bright colour all over before they were satisfied (*43* and *44*). Matthew, aged 8, had black cardboard and some gay vegetable netting. Nevertheless he added buttons for more variety (*45*). His older brother Noel has tried out two entirely different approaches, on cardboard and on wood. In the first one he has patiently built up areas of contrasting string textures (*46*) and in the other he has tried dividing up space by stretching string from one nail to another, afterwards colouring the shapes between with a felt-tip pen (*47*).

A group of 10-year-olds show a much more literal approach, using their string to draw animals, birds and flowers (*48-51*) but nevertheless filling the space well.

Twelve-year-old Katie has taken this pictorial theme a stage further, where the string textures are so much enjoyed that the duck's plumage is an excuse to show off patterns in string (*52*).

Equally sensitive are the rhythmic doodles of 12- to 15-year-old grammar school girls in Bermondsey who used a mixture of natural string and the coloured bits left over from a tie-dying session. Their shapes were lively but enormously enhanced by being cut out (the ground was yellowish strawboard) and remounted on a darker cardboard ground (*53-57*).

Figure *53* was made collectively by four girls working at opposite corners, all very much influenced by each other so that the result is a unity. They were quite happy to let their patterns grow out of the process of sticking a small area at a time, enjoying the contrast of natural and dyed areas of string as they went along.

It is a good idea when using white and natural coloured string, to let the younger children work on a gay coloured cardboard where possible. Cardboard can be dyed with coloured ink or covered with sticky coloured paper. While adults and young people may appreciate the limited colours of these string pictures in their varied tones and subtle shades, it is unlikely that small children will appreciate such subtlety. While they may enjoy the excercise uncritically, this enjoyment could be so much enhanced by brilliant grounds of orange, red, blue, green and purple. In the same way children love making patterns, sticking stones or twigs or seeds into bright coloured plasticine. This contrast of natural colour with brilliance can be delightful and right at this age and stage of artistic development.

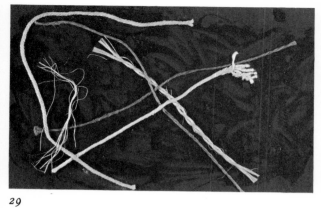

29

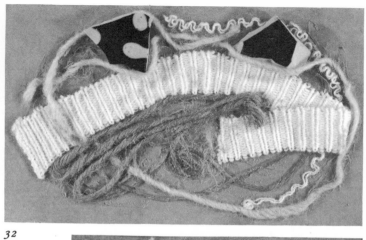

32

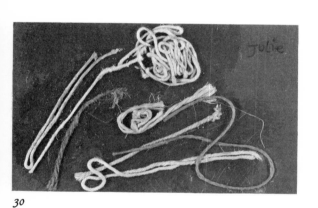

30

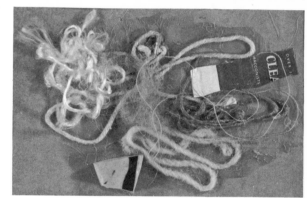

33

31

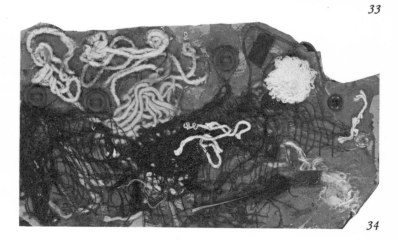

34

41

35

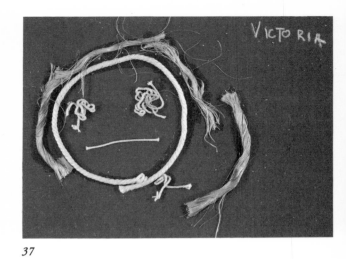

VICTORIA

37

36

38

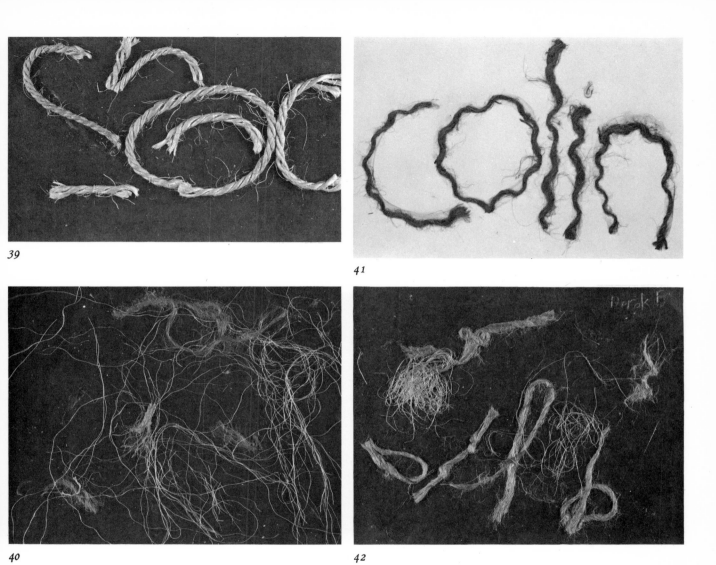

39

41

40

42

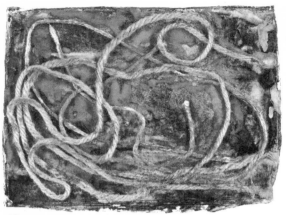

43

44

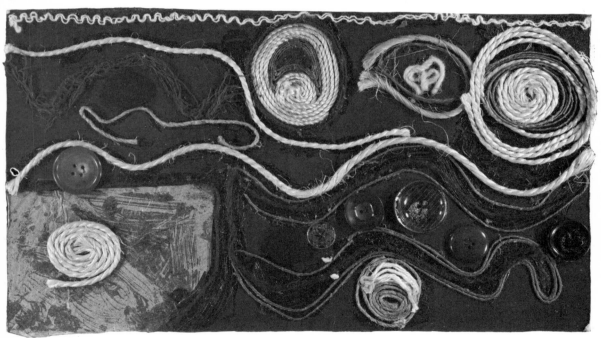

45

44

47

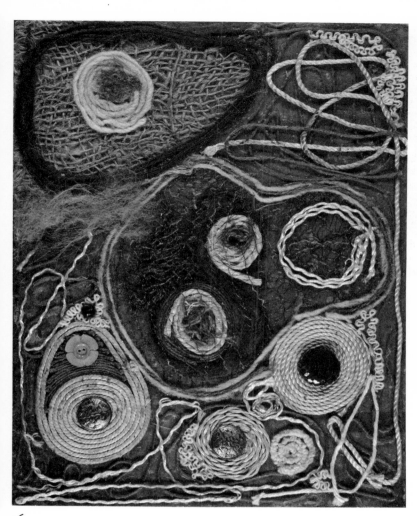

46

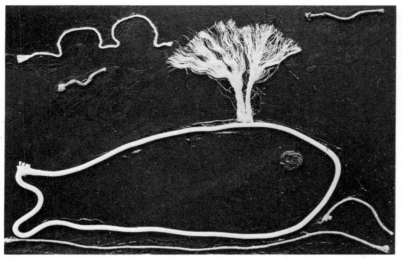

48

50

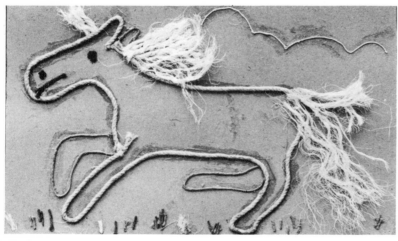

49

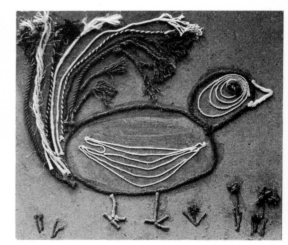

51

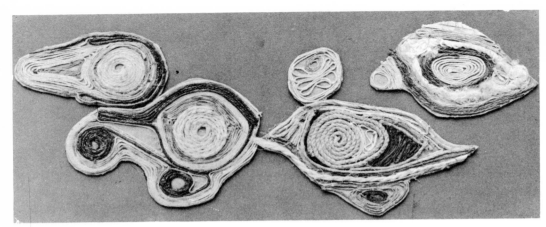

53

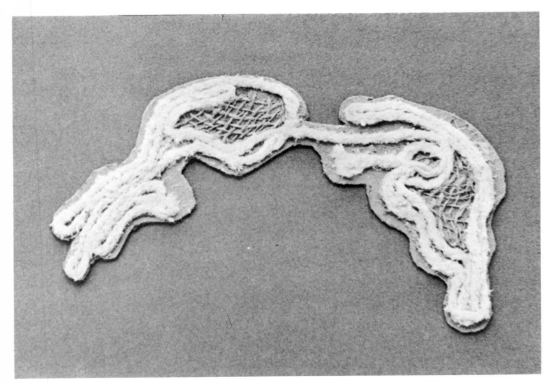

54

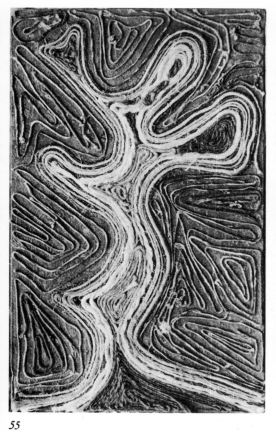

55

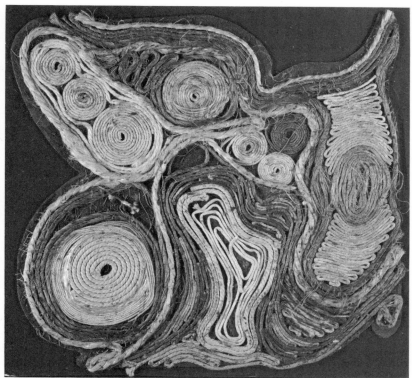

56

57

49

5   ABSTRACT AND IMAGINATIVE

The secondary school-age girls who made the abstract compositions in the last section show practical evidence of their pleasure and also their patience. These exercises, incidentally, were part of their school needlecraft lesson.

What other ways might one begin? Weaving students at a college of art played with variations in vertical and horizontal directions (58). A student at a college of education stuck down a curling piece of string and afterwards filled in the holes that resulted, using all the kinds of string she could find (59). Another expressed an idea of growth in a similar way, varying the pattern but keeping to one direction (60). A third student shows a tree growth in an abstract form—this could be either a section of the tree, its bark or the grain of its timber (61).

The circular theme in figure 62, by a student at a college of education, explores line doodling and space filling in yet another way.

The subject in figure 63 arose from the way the sisal string curled and suggested willow-herb and scattering seeds. Figures 64 and 65 are imaginary flowers and leaves, where the subject is very freely used to explore string textures.

Before selecting the string, but understanding its linear nature, doodling with string could be preceded by doodling a line with pen or pencil on paper to get the hand working in a rhythmic way. These ideas need not be rigidly copied in string but directions and ideas may grow from such a method of 'freeing up'. Better still perhaps, patterns in the air could be described with the arms and with the whole body, later to be interpreted and developed as a string composition. Gwyther Irwin's *Stringent* (66) and *Cordon Bleu* (108) may well have arisen from such a form of rhythmic doodling. Their subtlety and reservation are restful and stimulating.

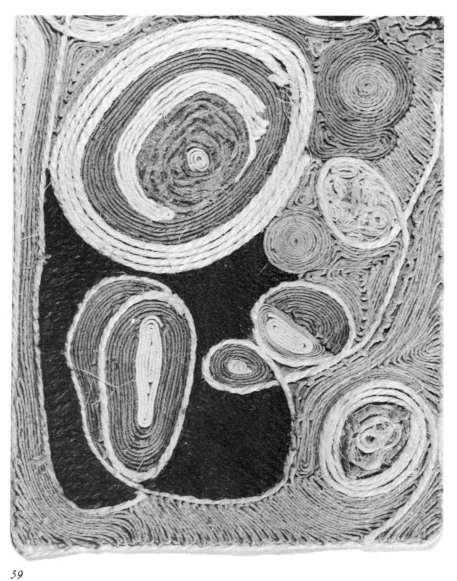

59

60

52

61

62

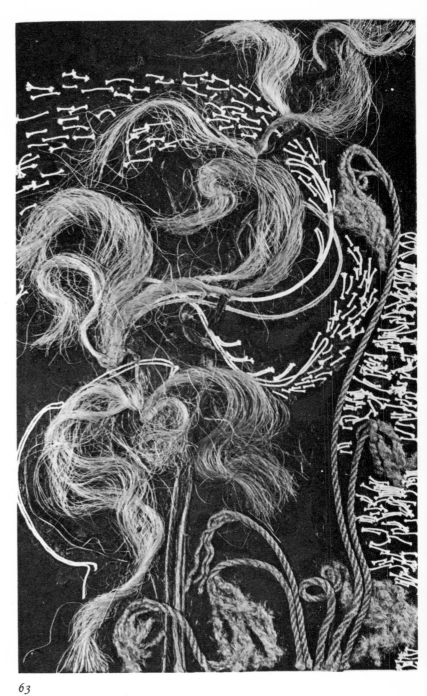

64

65

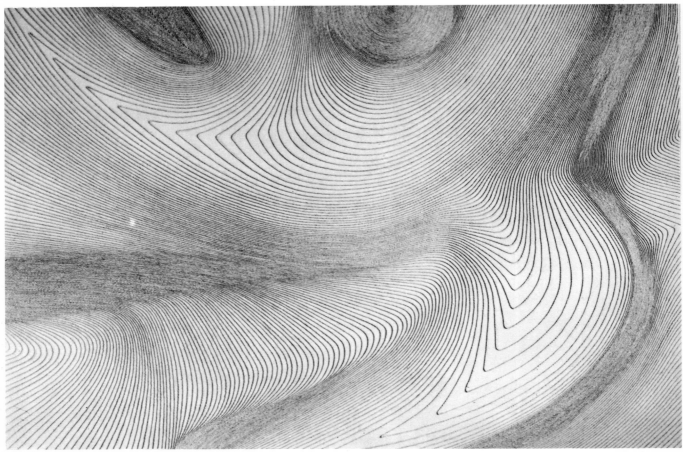

Rhythmic doodle by a 15 year old schoolgirl

6 STIMULI FROM NATURE AND ENVIRONMENT

Rhythmic doodling suggests an opposite approach. Abstract patterns have evoked glimpses of reality such as seeing pictures in the fire. The opposite is to study reality; simplifying and abstracting patterns from nature and environment. We have already produced patterns which remind us of recognisable themes; trees, leaves, flowers and seeds. Imagination can run down if it is not being recharged by observation. The analysis of pattern in the world around us is an infinite source of inspiration; for example, the bark of trees, bare twigs against the sky, sea-worn pebbles and chipped flints, grain of timber, oil on water, breaking surf, cart ruts in melted snow, flats lit up at night, the cell-structure of protozoa.

To observe effectively is an active process. We need to exclude all else and concentrate and analyse one small part. There are various ways of responding to what we see, but real observation has to be learnt.

67

68

69

70

71

Figure *67* shows a group of pebbles and *68* is an attempt to put down in line on paper the pattern they suggest. Similarly *69* shows fir-cones dropped in a heap and *70* is a line drawing simplifying their rhythms and patterns. Figure *71* is an abstract which could have come from either the pebbles or the fir-cones; a circular idea with variations on a circle has arisen. So observing the pebbles and fir-cones could result in the composition in figure *72*, a richer production than *59*, which arose simply from the doodling process. Whether or not the student who produced this particular composition was directly inspired by nature, this sort of observation can only enrich the observer, and build up a fund of ideas or pictorial vocabulary. This process in the end influences the quality of imaginative play.

72

73

74

Apart from describing patterns in space, other ways to respond or analyse would be to tear out shapes in paper (*74*), or cut up pieces of cheap cloth. Looking again at figure *72*, instead of drawing, circular shapes of vegetable netting of different kinds could be cut out and strands of thread stuck or sewn on to the background. Out of this an embroidery might arise. This particular example was inspired by sea-weed and carried out in overlapping net, but the feeling of the sea-weed has been abstracted from its commonplace appearance and re-interpreted (*73*).

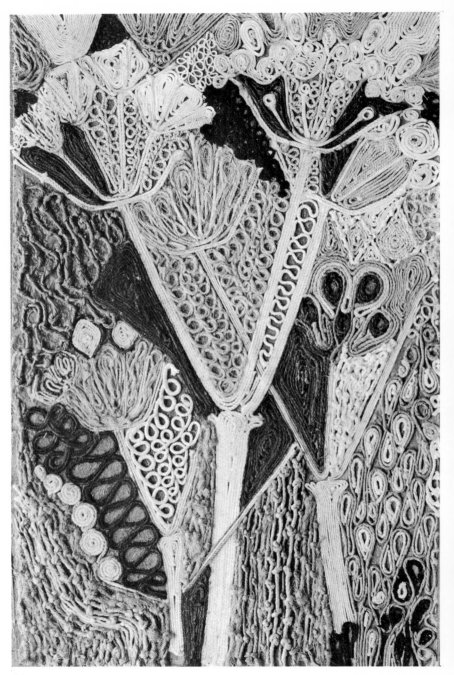

75

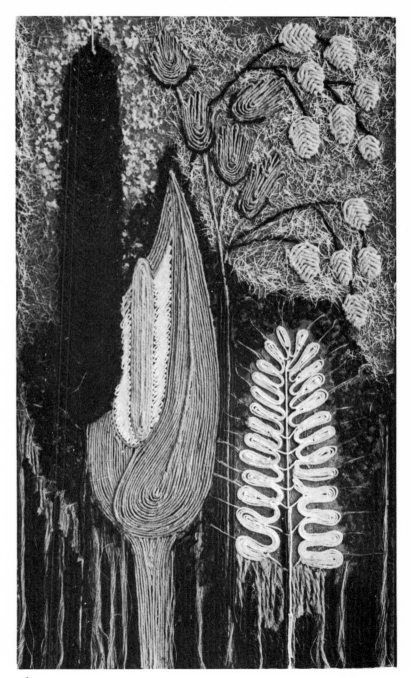

The student who produced figure 75 made a profound study of growth patterns of plants, flowers and trees in her own garden over the period of a year, inventing all manner of ways of depicting what she observed. Her interpretation of *Seedheads in String* is evidence of a developed sensitivity both to the subject and to the materials she was using. Figure 76 shows a similar sensitivity.

Microscope slides provide a source of fascinating patterns and rhythms:

77 Part of the life cycle of a tape worm
78 An imaginative interpretation of this tonal rhythmic pattern
79 A geological section
80 A string 'abstract' worked directly without an intermediate design
81 and 82 A primrose ovary enlarged, interpreted in line with a consequent string pattern in mind. This ultimate aim has influenced the line drawing—straight and knotty lines

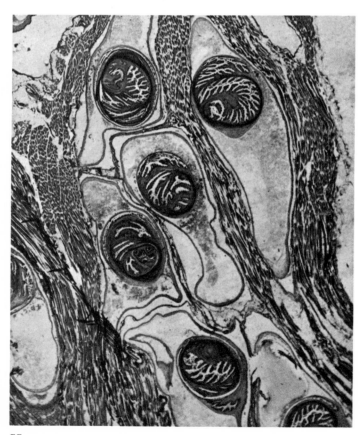

77

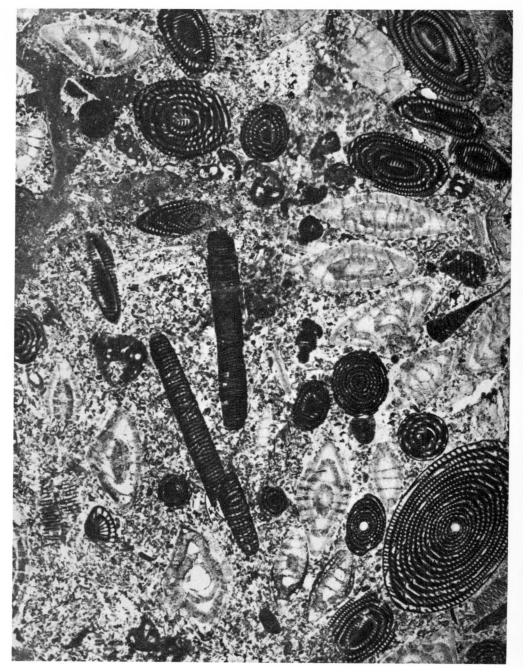

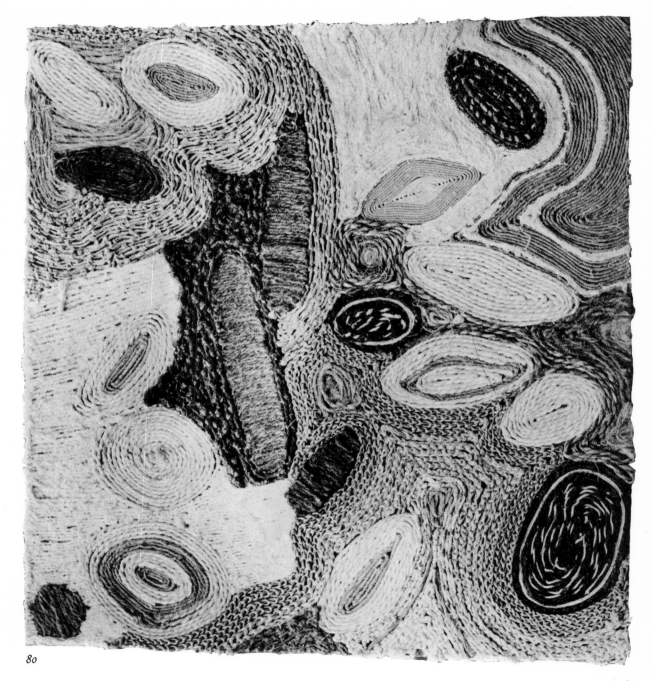

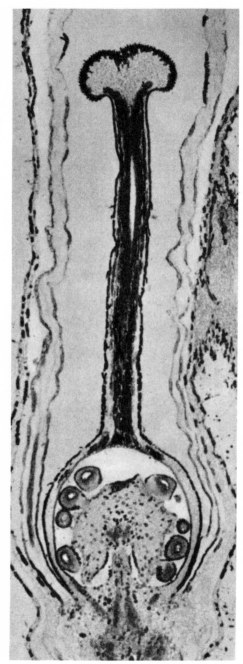

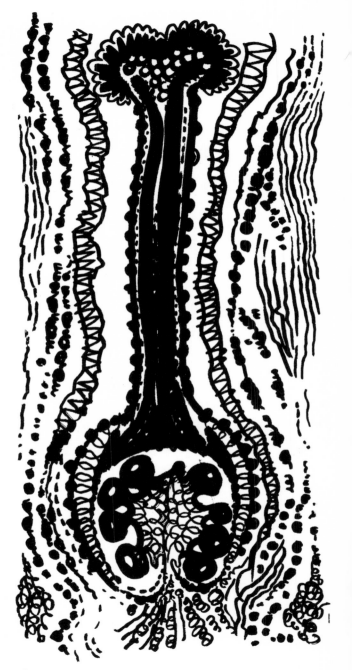

81

82

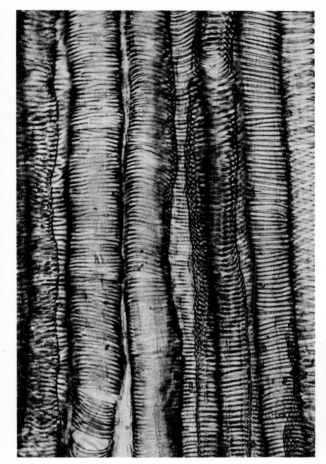

83

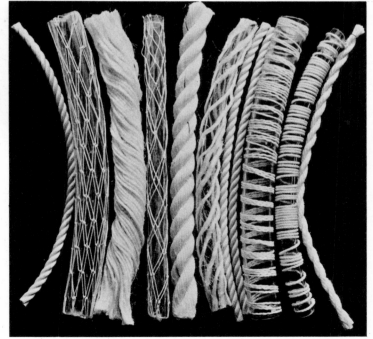

84

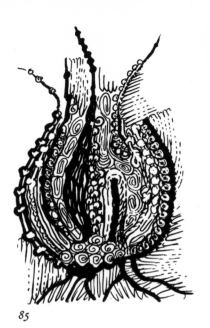

85

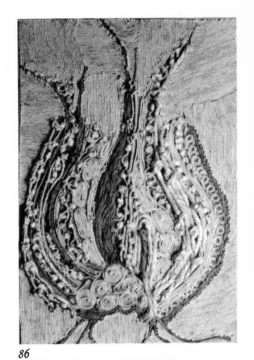

86

87

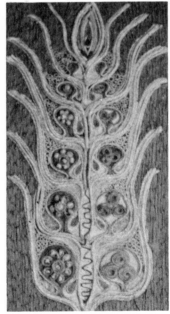

88

Similarly looking at an onion section, figure *85* might lead to figure *86*, and at an ear of wheat, figure *87* might lead on to figure *88*. This intermediate stage is suggested because ideas sometimes arise when there is no opportunity to embark on a major task, and a drawing or a pattern in torn paper can fix the experience often better than a photograph because the doing of it involves a struggle and involvement. The drawing does not have to be an accurate one, it is to serve as a reminder to oneself of what was seen.

89

Figures *89–92* are more pictorial in character.

90

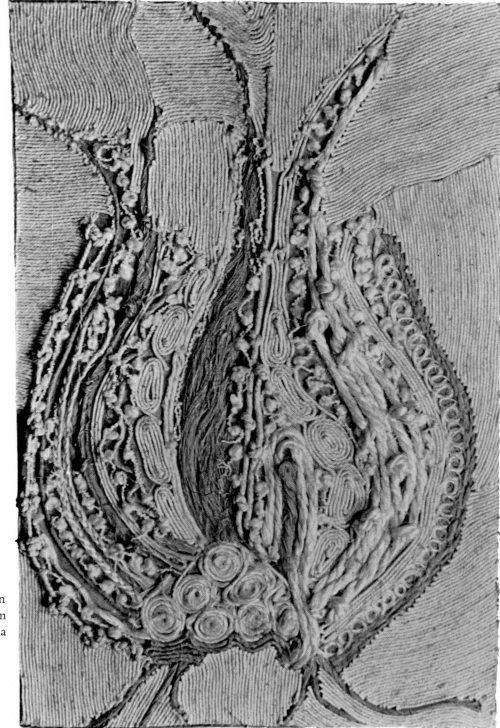

A free interpretation in string of an onion section made by a student at a College of Education

91

92

At this point it is very easy to become over-involved with the subject matter and the technique, and to turn out work that is merely complicated and clever. These examples show sensitive and lively interpretations of a primitive mask—the tufts of hair are an imaginative touch (*89*), still-life groups with bottles and fruit (*90* and *91*) and the triangular patterns of a sailing boat which come out crisply in continuous string (*92*).

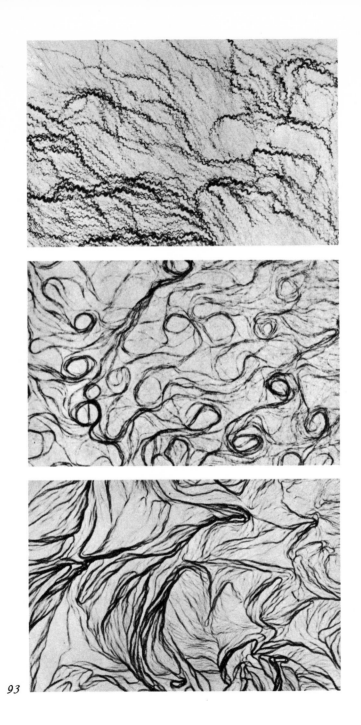

93

94

To illustrate further sources of stimuli, figure *93* is reminiscent of the pattern made by pulling jute apart (*15*)

Figure *94* shows twigs against the sky and the line drawing indicates how this could be interpreted in string

95 A rubbing from a worn paving stone. The stone was rubbed with candlewax on a sheet of thin white paper, afterwards flooded with liquid black paint which ran off the waxy parts

7 WHERE CAN IT LEAD?

The only way to produce work of any merit is to struggle with the problems and continually take up new challenges. The reason that string is suggested as a valuable medium is its cheapness and availability. It can also be used in such a variety of ways. In order to do ambitious work it is necessary to experiment in many ways first, even if many attempts en route are discarded.

What then can grow from these exercises? Much of the work illustrated in this book is by students of textiles, embroidery and weaving. The limitations in the colour of string can isolate and emphasise the problems of texture and tone pattern and colour within a limited range, in fact the basic principles of space-filling and design. Let us take some examples.

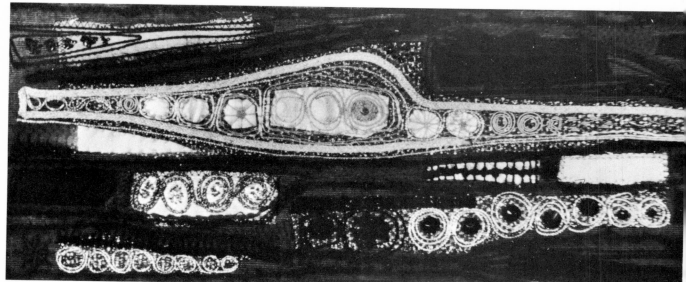

96

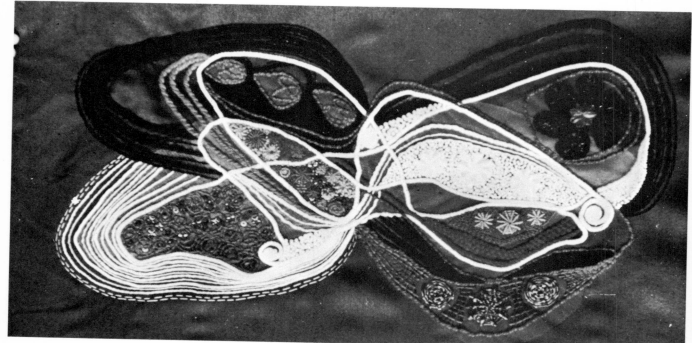

97

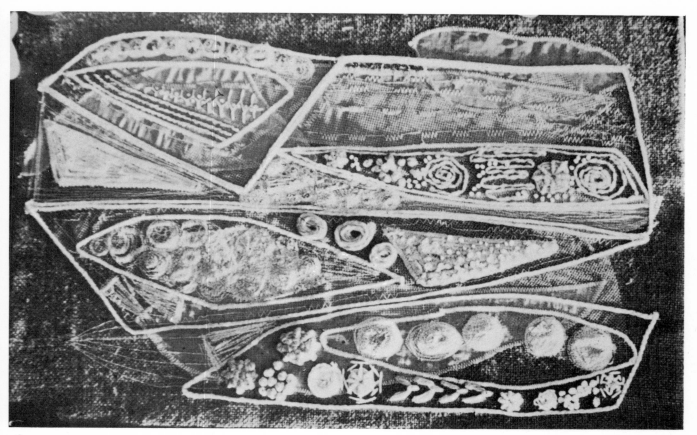

98

Gold Cell Structure (96) by Susan James shows what richness of colour can be achieved within a limited range with the addition of gold and silver threads to black and white. Her students work, figures *97* and *98*, show examples within other imposed limitations.

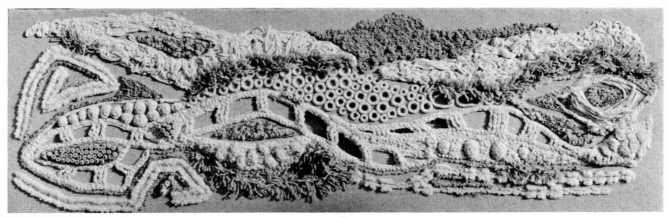

99

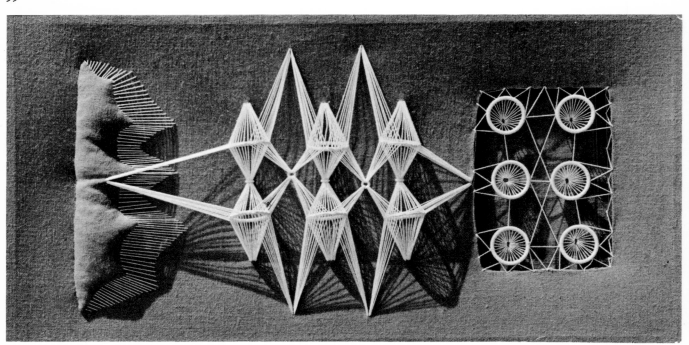

100

Elisa Rees subtly exploits the textures of wool and string in an almost colourless panel worked on two depths of natural hessian (burlap) (*99*). In the 3D panel she brings out the string to produce a delightful pattern echoed by its shadow and going back in depth. The background here is brilliant orange, setting off the white string (*100*).

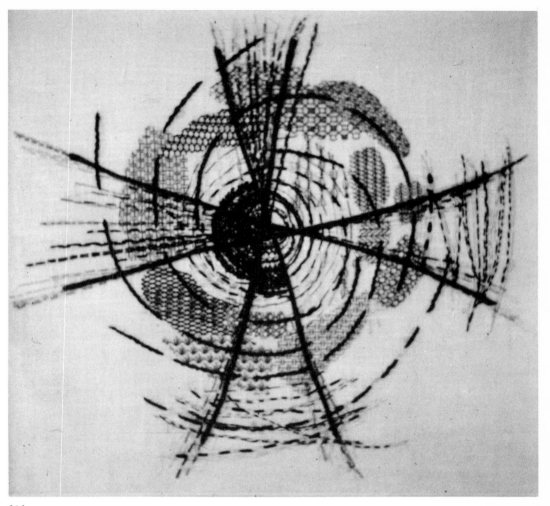

101

A student at a college of education made a study of The Cross in Design (*101*). This embroidery in black-work and pulled stitches was worked on a piece of very loosely woven linen and cotton mixture, approximately 30 in. × 36 in.

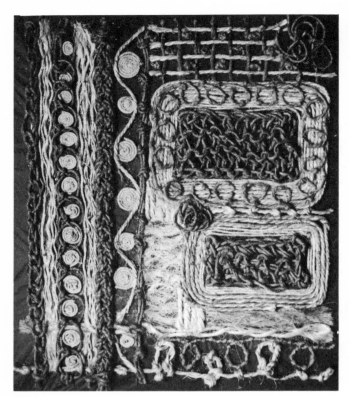

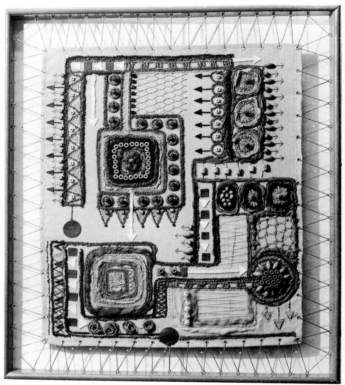

102

103

102 A string composition by a student at a college of education juxtaposed against another panel by Mrs Rees (*103*). The latter is carried out in threads and beads of brilliant red, purple and orange, the ground laced to a red frame, but in both the design approach is similar

104 A screen print on linen produced from a wax rubbing of the *Seedheads* composition (*75*). This was produced by the same student and was printed in shades of yellow and gold

105

106

Figures *105* and *106* are exercises by students at a college of art working on textural variety with warp and weft of the same grey threads, the ultimate aim being decorative hangings and textiles

107 An off-white canvas beach-bag designed by Gladys Lilley. This is enriched with appliqué of cord and string, also in off-white tones, exploiting textural quality in a circular design

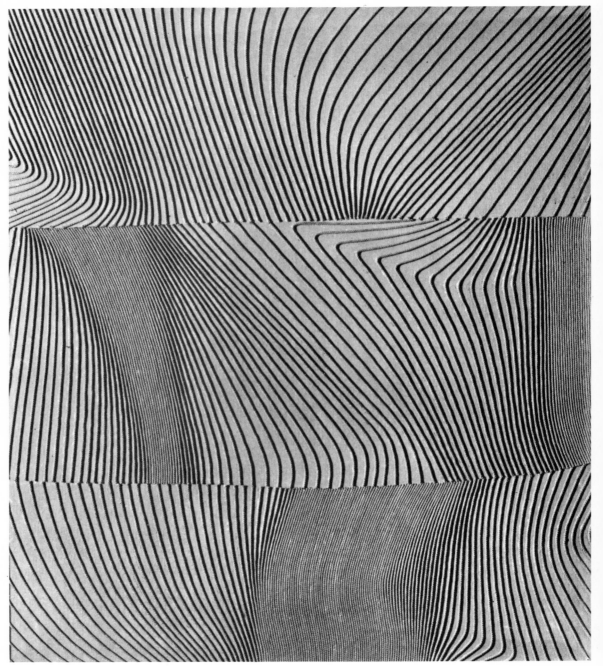

108

109

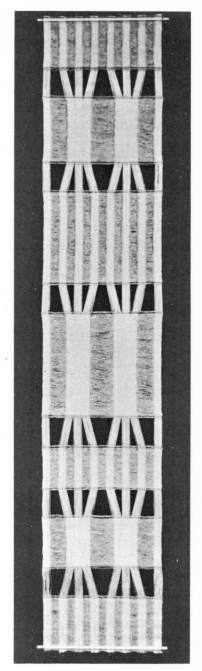

108 opposite Gwyther Irwin, technically a painter, has patiently stuck his fine cord string on to a canvas ground, producing an optical effect of depth, movement and peace

109–110 A decorative woven wall-hanging by Peter Collingwood in dark linen threads on a natural warp. His originality as a weaver owes much to continued experiment in a rich variety of media and techniques

110

111

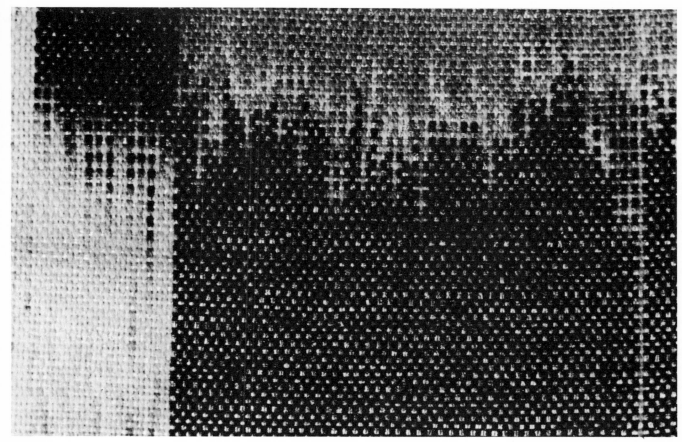

112

111 opposite Ruth Hurle, also a weaver, has playfully woven her string panel on to a linen warp, making subtle differences of shade and thickness

112 Ann Sutton's glistening wall-hanging. Transparent cellophane, woven on a tie-dyed warp, ingeniously shows the pattern of the warp through the shimmering surface of the weft

113 Coomacka Tree String collage on hessian (burlap) by the author

BIBLIOGRAPHY

Textile and Embroidery Design

Block Printing on Textiles   Janet Erickson, *Watson-Guptill New York*
The Technique of Woven Tapestry   Tadek Beutlich, *Batsford London, and Watson-Guptill New York*
Print Your Own Fabrics   Jutta Lammer, *Batsford London and Watson-Guptill New York*
Creative Textile Design: Thread and Fabric   Rolf Hartung, *Batsford London and Reinhold New York*
Inspiration for Embroidery   Constance Howard, *Batsford London and Branford Newtown Centre*
Handweaving Today   Ethel Mairet, *Faber and Faber London*

Inspiration from Natural Form

Forms and Patterns in Nature   Wolf and Strache, *Pantheon New York*
Form in Art and Nature   Georg Schmidt and others, *Basilius Press Basel and Heinman Imported Books New York*
Snow Crystals   W A Bentley and W J Humphreys, *Dover New York*
Life Under the Sea   Maurice Buston, *Spring Books Paul Hamlyn London*
Life Under the Microscope   Acadamician Otto Jirovec Dr Bedrich Boucek Professor Jiri Fiala, *Paul Hamlyn London*
Formen des Microkosmos   Carl Struwe, *Prestel-Verlag Munich*

Design and Creative Craft Education

Basic Design   Maurice de Saumarez, *Studio Vista London and Reinhold New York*
Mosaic-Making   Helen Hutton, *Batsford London and Reinhold New York*
The Nature of Design   David Pye, *Studio Vista London and Reinhold New York*
Creative Play Series   *Batsford London and Reinhold New York*
Dictionary of Creative Activity for School Use   Max Dimmack, *Macmillan London*
You Are An Artist   Fred Gettings, *Paul Hamlyn London*
Scribbling, Drawing, Painting   Wolfgang Grossinger, *Faber and Faber London*
Creative Crafts in Education   Seonid Robertson, *Routledge and Kegan Paul London*

SUPPLIERS IN GREAT BRITAIN

Adhesives

Marvin Medium, **Margos Ltd,** Woking, Surrey
Polycell and '*Heavyduty*' *Polycell,* **J Lines,** Tottenham Court Road, London W1
Evostik and *Copydex* from most big stationers
Unibond, Polybond, Bondcrete, Richafix, from builders' merchants
P.V.A. Medium from **George Rowney and Co,** 10 Percy Street, W1
Polymer Medium from **Reeves and Sons Ltd,** Lincoln Road, Enfield, Middlesex

Cardboard and strawboard

From all educational suppliers, printing firms, stationers and artists' suppliers,

E J Arnold & Sons Ltd, Butterley Street, Leeds 10, Yorkshire
George Rowney & Co Ltd, 10 Percy Street, London W 1
Reeves and Sons Ltd, Lincoln Road, Enfield, Middlesex
Dryad Ltd, 21 Bloomsbury Street, London WC 1, and Northgates, Leicester

Hardwood and plywood

From local timber merchants and 'Do-it-yourself' shops

Rope, string, canvas and hessians

Russell & Chapple, Monmouth Street, London WC 2
Mister Bosun's Locker, East Street, Chichester, West Sussex,
                and all yacht chandlers
Euston Asbestos, Euston Road, London NW 1 (large orders only)

Tarred string

From yacht chandlers, ironmongers and garden suppliers

Embroidery threads and materials

The Needlewoman, Regent Street, London W 1
Dryad Ltd, 21 Bloomsbury Street, London WC 1, and Northgates, Leicester

Metal threads

Toye, Kenning and Spencer Ltd, Regalia House, Red Lion Square, London WC 1

Schools should be encouraged to organise the collecting and storing of as much used string and rope as possible. These materials are not cheap to buy, but are easy to collect if sufficient time is allowed beforehand, and enough people are willing to help.

SUPPLIERS IN THE USA

Adhesives

Adhesives such as *Elmer's*, *Sobo*, and various other contact cements are generally available from hardware stores and builders' supply houses.

Cardboard and strawboard

Arthur Brown & Co, 2 West 46th Street, New York, N.Y. 10036
A. I. Friedman Inc, 25 West 45th Street, New York, N.Y. 10036
These two leading art suppliers publish mail order catalogues and make shipments throughout the country.

Hardboard and plywood

These materials are available from local timber merchants (lumber yards) and 'Do-it-Yourself' shops.

Rope, string, canvas and hessians (burlap)

Hardware and stationery stores stock rope and string. Fabric stores carry burlap. Rope, string and canvas may be purchased at marine equipment and supply houses.

Tarred string

Tarred string may be purchased from marine supply stores, hardware stores and garden suppliers.

Embroidery threads and materials

Joan Toggitt Ltd, 52 Vanderbilt Avenue, New York, N.Y.

INDEX OF MATERIALS